The Way Out

or

How Electronic Revenue Credits Can:
End the Debt Crisis,
Open Government and Restart
the Economy

by

C. P. Klapper

Also by C. P. Klapper

~

The Washington Poems
Sonnets for the Spanish
The Fallacies of Atheism
Popular Capitalism

The Way Out

or

How Electronic Revenue Credits Can End the Debt Crisis, Open Government and Restart the Economy

by

C. P. Klapper

The Lion and Lambda Press
New Brunswick, NJ

ISBN-13: 978-1-934882-04-7 (paperback)

Library of Congress Control Number: 2013921043

Printed in the United States of America.

Dedication

To my fellow Unheard Americans

Preface

In *Popular Capitalism*, I present a more general solution to the root problem of our political economy, namely the problem of poverty. In the realm of political discourse, however, there are other problems which are made to seem more pressing. To those families pressed under the weight of grinding poverty, it is hard to find any problem more immediate, yet there we have it: little interest in the root and an obsession with the leaves. So to those families, I offer my apologies for this diversion, offering the solace that their needs are more likely to be addressed, and with fewer reservations, after politicians are shown a way out of the pit they have dug for us.

C. P. Klapper
Piscataway, NJ

Table of Contents

The Deepening Pit of Debt

I n a strange bit of misdirection, the extent of federal debt is referred to as a ceiling, rather than as a floor. Indubitably, this is intended to give the impression that debt is something to which we aspire, rather than something into which we have sunk. Hopefully, there are few of us who are still manipulated by such cheap rhetorical tricks, and hopefully there will be none once this deception is exposed. Let me express plainly the truth which the phrase *debt ceiling* is meant to obscure: *debt* is a bad thing and more debt is worse.

One reason more debt is worse is that it saps our ability to pay it back. To *service* the debt, as payment of interest is delicately put, we have to pay money just to stay at the same level. If we do not have the money, then we have to dig deeper, to lower the floor of our pit of debt, by borrowing more money. Thus we have a deepening pit of debt, from which escape is harder with each further descent. All the while, the revenue used to pay the interest on the debt is taken from sources which are increasingly in danger of being depleted. We end up taxing the people onerously, not to raise the debt floor, not even to keep from lowering the debt floor, but only to slow further descent into the pit of debt.

We may try to extricate ourselves by reducing the amount we spend on other things, but eventually we realize that the interest on the debt is swallowing up all of our savings from foregoing luxuries, then our savings from foregoing essential tools for our productive tasks, and finally our deprivations from foregoing what we need to survive. If we can gain a foothold by paying off some of the principal, we have to be careful not to then slip with a shortfall in revenue or an unexpected expense. Yet we can never be careful enough to avoid the inevitable. Especially when our tools are in disrepair and our bellies are empty, there will always be shortfalls in revenue and unexpected expenses. Austerity brings the mistakes that will cause us to slip back down from every slight ascent. For as long as we insist on working within the pit of debt, we are doomed to stay there.

Yet it is out of the depths that we gain wisdom. Once we realize that the pit is what traps us, a way out then appears. We look outside the pit to see other ways of fulfilling our obligations, ways which do not involve interest payments. We take a break from desperation and go to the store to return that ill-fitting garment we got from a well-meaning relative. We get on a line and finally meet with a clerk at the returns counter. There we find out that we will not be able to sell the shirt back to the store. Instead, the store will issue a credit for us to buy something else. We amaze the clerk by thanking them profusely for what hundreds of customers have cursed them that very day. Why? Because we have seen the way out, with the clerk our unwitting guide.

We call our creditors and tell them our plight and our offer. We will offer them a credit for them to buy our products in exchange for releasing us from our debt with them. Maybe these are things we make, quilts or bookcases, or maybe they are so many hours of our labor at a reasonable hourly rate. We set aside some time to earn our daily keep, of course, but we are able to work off our debt by fulfilling orders from customers and clients we might not otherwise have had. We climb out of the pit of debt and vow never to return.

Brilliant enough for you, you might say, but how does this help our country? The answer is there, right in front of us: taxes or, in general, revenue is what our government receives for what it "sells". Our Treasury can issue the federal equivalent of store credits, made more flexible and capable through modern technology, for an entity to "buy" a fulfillment of tax obligations, as well as items which are directly sold, such as passports, or services which are now indirectly sold, such as delivery of letters and packages.

Electronic Revenue Credits

The federal government may not be known for its productive capabilities, or for offering goods and services to a free market, but it does take in revenue and that is enough for it to issue its own take on the store credit. Instead of returned merchandise, there are expenditures of all sorts. Instead of store credits being used to buy other merchandise, there are revenue credits used to pay taxes and fines, purchase stamps or even to buy merchandise available for sale at federal facilities. We might think this a huge undertaking until we realize that this much has already been implemented with coins and has been, in the past, with paper currency.

The difference in what we are proposing here is using this mechanism to pay back the federal debt.

Because of the immense size of that debt, coinage for general circulation will be insufficient, and currency in paper, though feasible and legal, would require some time in preparing the plates and acquiring the additional stock for production. Electronic means afford us a quick way of creating revenue credits, with only the writing of some straightforward software required as preparation. Thus we have the Electronic Revenue Credit, or ERC for short.

At this point, we have to consider the operation of the ERC and the costs which might be involved. If the ERC is to be a currency in general circulation, we would have to be concerned with the logistics of how they are transferred into and out of regular accounts and with preventing counterfeiting during that process. Indeed, these difficulties suggest that we might want to avoid placing the ERC in general circulation, restricting its owners to the two necessary for its use: the Treasury and the Federal Reserve as central bank. Doing so has the additional benefit of preventing the alien ownership of a sovereign financial instrument, a danger to which we are currently exposed by federal debt instruments.

The ERC would then be a reserve asset passed between the Treasury and the Federal Reserve, without the intermediary of an open market committee and without an obligation being made to a foreign power or an international lender. Thus, when the Treasury issues a check and it is presented to be drawn from the account of the Treasury at the Federal Reserve, the Treasury supplements any deficiency in its balance by selling ERCs to the Federal Reserve. Conversely, when checks are paid to the Treasury, any excess balance can be used to buy ERCs back from the Federal Reserve.

To put meat to the bones of this description, let us say that the ERC is denominated at one thousand dollars. Then, if John Q. Public deposits his federal pay check of $1,000 in his bank, his bank credits his account $1,000, pending clearance of the check. His bank then hands the check up the chain to, say, its federal reserve bank, which then credits John's bank $1,000, again pending clearance. Eventually, the check for $1,000 reaches the Federal Reserve, where we will do things a little differently than at present. In our case, the Federal Reserve will buy an ERC from the Treasury with $1,000 of its own ledger money and then withdraw that $1,000 to give to the federal reserve bank, to give to John's bank and, finally, to John's account, clearing the check. The Federal Reserve has one more ERC and John has an additional $1,000 of ledger money in his account.

In the other direction, Sally R. Taxpayer writes a $1,000 check for her income tax and sends it to the IRS. The IRS deposits Sally's check into the general account of the Treasury and the Federal Reserve credits the Treasury $1,000 pending the check clearing. The federal reserve bank for Sally's bank then credits the Federal Reserve, again pending her check being cleared, and sends it to her bank. Sally's bank then withdraws $1,000 from her account, which then works its way back up the chain until it reaches the Federal Reserve. This money is set for deposit into the account of the Treasury, but we will also do this a little differently. In one deft movement, the $1,000 will be deposited and then used, on behalf of the Treasury, to buy an ERC back from the Federal Reserve. The Federal Reserve has one less ERC and Sally has $1,000 less money in her account.

Note that, in our examples, the ERCs held by the Federal Reserve and the changes in the bank accounts move in the same direction. This is because the ERCs represent negative value in the Treasury. Another word for this negative value is *deficit*. We can therefore think of ERCs as little bits of federal deficits being shuttled back and forth between the Treasury and the Federal Reserve. They flow out from the Treasury for daily deficits and flow back in for daily surpluses.

We can also think of the federal debt in a similar fashion. The debt is composed of deficits which have been deferred until some later date. At an earlier time, the Treasury did not have enough money in its account to pay for the checks it issued, so it issued some debt instruments (Treasuries) to whomever would buy them. It then deposited the proceeds of that sale in its account so that the checks could be cashed. When these Treasuries mature, the Treasury can pay the principal with what can be viewed as a surplus, the cash currently held in its general account. If the surplus is a true surplus, and not simply a net positive value over a small region of time and space, then there is no unmatched deficit elsewhere to cancel the surplus out. On the other hand, if it is merely temporary and local, it can still be thought of as a surplus canceling out an existing deficit, but with the new Treasuries as a flood of deficit reinforcements overwhelming its paltry defense. In any case, the surplus , for all of that, cancels out a deficit.

The mechanisms of ERCs and of Treasuries are, in this sense, similar. If a government runs a surplus and shows a positive balance in its account, it can cancel out the deficit represented by an ERC or by a Treasury. Two crucial differences remain, however. An ERC is free of interest, making payments on principal much easier for the federal government than for a Treasury. Also, debt matures when stipulated, which may turn out to be at an inconvenient time for a variety of less than predictable reasons. The Treasury may not have money in its account; the federal government may not be able to stay open if its pays the principal just then; or those pressures and the expense of the debt may make an increase in indebtedness both urgent and politically infeasible. Yet an ERC can be issued at any time, has no term and need not be replaced with a copy of itself.

Climbing Out of Debt

W e have just described how old deficits in either form, Treasury debt or ERCs, can be canceled out by surpluses. They are also exchangeable by virtue of funds created by one being used to destroy the other. For our purposes, though, there is only one desired direction: replacing Treasury debt with ERCs.

Doing so is simple and straightforward. Paying the principal of a Treasury when it matures can be done with a check, as for other expenses. The check clears in the same way as before, the Federal Reserve buying ERCs with its ledger money, withdrawing that ledger money from the general account of the Treasury in order to clear the check. At the end of the day, Treasury debt has been replaced by ERCs held by the Federal

Reserve and ledger money has been transferred from the Federal Reserve to the holder of the check, who then is free to withdraw cash from those funds or to keep them on deposit. If we consider the coupon to be part of the debt, then the ERCs replace the debt in its interest payments when the coupon checks are cleared.

There is no need to force the matter in buying Treasuries before they mature. Using ERCs at maturity, for servicing the debt and for any other daily deficits, is sufficient to stop the descent into deeper debt and to allow a gradual ascent out of the pit. The federal debt cannot grow larger, will indeed shrink, with this plan, thereby resolving the debt crisis, finally and completely.

Now will come questions from some who like to inject ignorant fears laced with seeming authority. I am speaking of the inflation-phobes, for whom every small increase in the money supply raises hyper-inflationary specters of Weimar Germany, with wheelbarrow wraiths to carry the cash. In "Popular Capitalism", I completely debunk the erroneous assertions upon which they base their hysteria, so there is no need to go into much detail here. There is, however, a gap in the exposition of ERC handling which it behooves us to fill in here, lest these fear-mongers be given an opening.

The gap in question has to do with the ledger money the Federal Reserve uses to buy and sell ERCs. You will recall that the Federal Reserve bought an ERC with its ledger money and got ledger money by selling an ERC. Where the Federal Reserve gets ledger money to purchase an ERC, and what it does with the ledger money it receives from selling an ERC, is key to understanding what effects ERC transactions have on the supply of money held by the public and thus key to determining if there are or might be any inflationary or deflationary effects.

First, if the Federal Reserve purchases ERCs with old money recently in the hands of the public, say from the sale of reserve assets, it would not have added to the public money supply in the complete transaction. That transaction would have simply transferred money from the asset purchaser to the account where the check was deposited. The other parts of the transaction have a clear purpose, but no effect on the supply of money held by the public. The Treasury has granted a new claim on its future revenue, embodied in the ERC it sold, in exchange for the goods or services it bought with its check. The Federal Reserve exchanged one reserve asset for another: the one it sold for the ERC it bought.

In the second case, the Federal Reserve takes money out of the hands of the public on behalf of the Treasury and, through its sale of an ERC back to the Treasury, adds that money to its own (Federal Reserve) ledger, reducing the public money supply. The Treasury, for its part, has one less $1,000 draw on its future revenue. There are two sub-cases to consider, depending upon how the corresponding ERC purchase was executed. If we view this as a combined transaction with the same ERC purchased with new money, there is no change in the public money supply, but also no exchange of a reserve asset for an ERC. If we view this as a combined transaction with the same ERC having been purchased with money from the sale of Treasuries, there is a reduction in the public money supply and in the Treasuries held by the Federal Reserve.

The only remaining case is where the Federal Reserve will not or cannot sell a reserve asset which is not an ERC. This is the only case where the public money supply increases. This case occurs whenever there is a deliberate decision by the Federal Reserve to increase the public money supply, say as a stimulus, or when it has converted all of its reserve assets to ERCs. Since federal debt instruments held by the Federal Reserve are a major component of its reserve assets, depletion is unlikely to occur much before the last Treasury matures.

Even if some Treasuries mature when they are still held by the Federal Reserve, the public money supply need not be increased. For each thousand dollars of principal from such Treasuries, the Federal Reserve can use a thousand dollars in its existing ledger money to buy an ERC. The Treasury can then use that money to pay the principal, so that the thousand dollars of ledger money returns to the Federal Reserve, where it can be recycled to claim the next thousand dollars of principal from other matured bonds it holds. The ledger money of the Federal Reserve is simply a catalyst for transforming Treasuries into ERCs and therefore never gets into the public money supply.

It is worth noting that the reason for no new money being needed to retire Treasuries held by the Federal Reserve is that the money was created to purchase them in the first place. A similar assertion applies to the Treasuries being sold off by the Federal Reserve, but here the Treasuries held as reserve assets are sold to reclaim the money used to purchase them. However, since prices change, the proceeds on their sale might be more or less than the money used to purchase them. This is another factor which the Federal Reserve must consider in its decision to create ledger money or to sell Treasuries in order to buy ERCs. If the market price for its Treasuries is too low, it could wait until their price rises or they mature, expanding the money supply and stimulating the economy in the meantime.

Wrapping up the loose ends of our discussion, we consider what happens when the Federal Reserve stops converting existing reserve assets into ERCs, as this will be the situation after all of the federal debt is retired. However created, the new ledger money is added to the public money supply and, in the aggregate with the revenue being subtracted from the public money supply, constitutes the running deficit of the federal government. Without a backlog of deficits from a federal debt, there can be no expectation of more deficits than surpluses in the future and hence there can be no expectations of future increases in the fiscal money supply. Therefore there can be no inflationary expectations from the mere fact of creating ledger money to purchase ERCs. Any inflation would then have to come from the way in which the ledger money is created.

At present, the way to create this ledger money is for the Federal Reserve to back it with reserve assets, which would then be the ERCs, as it has issued Federal Reserve Notes. This analogy gives us another name for the ERC process. *Deficit monetizing*, like the *debt monetizing* of the Federal Open Market Committee, converts a fiscal state into a reserve asset. The purpose is the same, whatever the type of reserve asset: to avert a bank run. That risk comes because the banks create debt money with their loans, which eventually becomes ledger money in the system, but lack the fiscal money in currency needed for total withdrawals.

In other words, private banks expand the money supply with loans and thereby create inflation. Rather than slandering our plan to get out of sovereign debt, inflation-phobes should join us in urging higher reserve requirements to restrict the creation of private debt money. Such a policy would be an improvement in general, as it would dampen the cyclical effects of lender confidence and its ebb and flow. Eventually, it would bring us to a political economy which is freed from debt, but public and private.

Keeping Government Open

P olitical posturing of all kinds and from all standpoints is greatly aided by a crisis. One side can stand on the side of justice, another on the side of law, and each can be heroes to their political machine, villains to the adepts of the other machine. They can point to polls or to reason, whichever better confirms their position and, when all crashes around them, they can blame the other side and only their side will believe them. That is what they are after, though they will indignantly deny it, each claiming they care about the people. Yet the plain truth of the matter is that the only ones hurt by this exercise are the people.

One form of hurt which has become popular of late, probably because the class affected is relatively small and of fairly uniform allegiance, is shutting down the federal government or, more correctly, partially shutting down the federal government, as a complete shutdown would also end the posturing. We couldn't have that, now could we? How else could the one side claim to have defended the victims without actually defending them? How could the other side claim no responsibility if they are not given the opportunity to volley the blame back over the net? A literal game of shame, that.

The good news is that, by removing the debt crisis with the ERC, we have removed at least one path to political posturing. The better news is that a few other paths can be removed, including the budget crisis, the spending crisis and the tax crisis. The ERC is, at root, a device of great flexibility and, above all else, crises abhor flexibility. While the federal sovereign debt is composed of deadlines – principal or interest must be paid now or default will forever condemn you – as also the budget and its tax and spending components, ERCs have no deadlines and no dire consequences. Not enough money today? No problem! Just pay when you can. With such a laid-back attitude, an ERC crisis is impossible.

Thus, if we could replace the budget with some other process compatible with the ERC, we could then eliminate the crises used to close government. This may seem like wishful thinking but it so happens that just such a process is described in Article I, Section 9, Clause 7 of the Constitution of the United States:

No Money shall be drawn from the Treasury, but in Consequence of Appropriations made by Law; and a regular Statement and Account of the Receipts and Expenditures of all public Money shall be published from time to time.

Note that the word "budget" does not appear in this clause. In fact, the word "budget" is nowhere even mentioned in the Constitution. What is described is a casual reporting of the "Receipts and Expenditures" of the Treasury, which correspond to revenue and checks in the ERC process. The only requirement in the clause is that there be appropriations legislation to authorize the Treasury checks in the first place. That is it. Nothing about an annual accounting. Nothing about setting tax or spending levels. Just give a report every so often.

So what does a budget accomplish for Congress which a pay-as-you-go process does not? In a word, *logrolling*. If laws are passed on principle but lack support for the practical matter of paying for them, then the Constitution would have them languish in their unfunded state until and unless there is that support. Logrolling circumvents this requirement by sharing support of appropriations bills. The budget process formalizes logrolling and makes it a requirement. Either all appropriations bills are passed or none are.

This requirement of the budget process for total logrolling introduces rigidities which provoke crises. All it takes is one law for which sufficient support is not sharable, either on principle or as a political necessity, and the budget process is brought to a screeching halt. Then, when the inevitable happens with a budget crisis, self-righteous bores can join the fun, posturing as pillars of responsibility who defend the budget process from those with radical ideas of representing the causes that got them elected. Of course, nobody shows any desire to defend honest representation or the legislative process from the budget. That would end the charade.

So we the people need to take matters into our own hands and create a furor over the corrupt dealings in Congress, targeting their main vehicle: the budget. Let us speak with one voice against the political machines and their charade. Let us demand an end to the budget and insist that the federal debt be replaced by the ERC.

If we are successful, only those laws with full support will have money spent on their implementation. If we are successful, the money spent on any one law will have no bearing on the money spent on other laws. If we are successful, the total money spent and the total revenue collected over a year will have no relationship with themselves or anything else. If we are successful, the casual pace of "from time to time" will be honored. If we are successful, no crises will be manufactured and therefore, if we are successful, the federal government will stay open doing just what the people want, no more, no less.

Starting the Economy

I n "Popular Capitalism", I present my vision for a political economy which does not require starting and does not fear ending of production or employment. However, such is not the current state of affairs. It will not even be the state of affairs if we have the ERC, though that instrument will enable us to implement popular capitalism. We are far from a world where we do not need to concern ourselves with starting or re-starting the economy.

On the other hand, long-term private lending, which I excoriate in my larger work, is available for our use in the present necessity. Thus, the apparatus of this lending can stay in place, allowing its operators to turn its levers, as is their custom, and to do what they can to help in the effort. Now is neither the time nor the place to make enemies of institutions which still wield power enough to stall the economy indefinitely. It is better to have them on our side, expanding the debt money supply so that the expansion of the fiscal money supply can be lessened.

For that is the means of restarting the economy: the increase of the supply of money for consumption or production. Whether the new money comes from bank loans or maturing bonds is not as important as there being new money. Whether the new money is sent first to the businesses who then pass it on to their workers in wages, or is sent first to the people who then pass it on to the businesses they patronize, is not a great concern as long as, in the end, workers are paid, shoppers buy and businesses produce.

The ERCs, though, are important in themselves because they allow increases in the fiscal money supply, both past and present, to be actuated, to be currently effective. The federal debt does not. Indeed, the federal debt is designed to be a way of putting off payments to a fixed point in the future. The advertising slogan "Buy Now. Pay Later." perfectly describes the federal debt.

By contrast, ERCs allow the federal government to pay now for its current expenses without future obligations. What gets put off, instead, is the exercise of the credit with which the payment was made. In the indefinite and possibly infinite interim, that credit forms the basis of the money created by the expense, at the time it was spent. This immediacy assures an immediate fiscal stimulation of the economy which the federal debt, by its very nature, is incapable of providing.

The ERC thus provides another way to restart the economy. This is sorely needed when private bank lending can no longer be prompted by monetary policy, as is currently the case. Indeed, quantitative easing (QE) has been the primary means of expanding the money supply for the last several years and, true to its name, its effect has been modest. The ERC provides an alternative way of expanding the money supply which is as capable of being fine-tuned as QE – through the mix of money creation and conversion of assets to ERCs – but with the reduction of the federal debt. QE merely changes ownership of the federal debt, so the ERC is needed to resolve the debt crisis and relieve the burden placed on investment markets in accommodating new federal debt. By ending the creation of new federal debt, the ERC enables QE to be applied to existing debt and therefore to be more effective in helping to restart the economy.

The expansion of the money supply from both the ERC and QE then provides the impetus needed for an effective stimulus. In addition, the ERC facilitates the spending decisions of Congress, regardless of whether those decisions affect the demand or supply side of the financial economy. This widens the scope of the stimulus from the narrower supply-side approach of QE, which funnels its new money only to investors. This broader introduction of new money prompts a full stimulus that encourages (on the demand side) and enables (on the supply side) businesses and individuals to secure new loans which are, themselves, new money, specifically, *debt money*. Thus, the ERC is the linchpin of the policies with which the federal government could generate an inflationary stimulus on a large enough scale to restart the economy.

Conclusion

N ow that we have a way out of the current collection of crises, we need to impel Congress to take that path. There are, I am certain, others who are better suited to devising political strategies and stratagems to accomplish this goal. Nonetheless, I can provide a point of contact which we can use to coordinate our efforts once those of you who are "in the know" have reached a critical mass. That point of contact will be at the web domain promoting popular capitalism:

http://www.popular-capitalist.org

I hope to hear from you there and to hear of your efforts in getting our government to take this way out.

www.ingramcontent.com/pod-product-compliance
Lightning Source LLC
Chambersburg PA
CBHW021338290326
41933CB00038B/964